Wood

Katie Dicker

Published by Evans Brothers Limited
2A Portman Mansions
Chiltern Street
London W1U 6NR

© Evans Brothers Limited 2009

Produced for Evans Brothers Limited by
White-Thomson Publishing Ltd

Printed in China by New Era Printing Co. Ltd
Printed on chlorine-free paper from sustainably managed sources.

Educational consultant: Sue Palmer MEd FRSA FEA
Project manager: Katie Dicker
Picture research: Amy Sparks
Design: Balley Design Limited
Creative director: Simon Balley
Designer/Illustrator: Andrew Li

For Charlie

British Library Cataloguing in Publication Data

Dicker, Katie
   Woods. - (Out and about) (Sparklers)
   1. Forests and forestry - Juvenile literature
   I. Title
   333.7'5

ISBN: 978 0 2375 3876 7

Contents

Woodland visit

Follow me!

Come for a walk in the wood!

Changing seasons

In winter, the trees are sprinkled with snow.

Wheee!

bluebells

In spring, a wood is full of flowers.

Look up!

tall tree

These leaves are green in summer.

8

In autumn, they fall to the ground.

9

What animals can YOU see?

Tree textures

big hug!

What does a tree trunk *feel* like?

What different bark textures can you find?

bark rubbing

What would it *feel* like

to live in a tree trunk?

Woodland home

These foxes live in a burrow.

What other creatures call

the wood their home?

Nuts and seeds

Tasty!

Why do squirrels store nuts and seeds in the autumn?

How many pine cones can YOU collect?

19

Using wood

tree house

Pull!

Strong wood is good for making things.

We plant trees to replace the wood that we use.

Notes for adults

Sparklers books are designed to support and extend the learning of young children. The **Food We Eat** titles won a Practical Pre-School Silver Award and the **Body Moves** titles won a Practical Pre-School Gold Award. The books' high-interest subjects link in to the Early Years curriculum and beyond. Find out more about Early Years and reading with children from the National Literacy Trust (www.literacytrust.org.uk).

Themed titles

Wood is one of four **Out and About** titles that encourage children to explore outdoor spaces. The other titles are:

Park   **Garden**   **Seaside**

A CD to accompany the series (available from Evans Publishing Group tel 020 7487 0920 or email sales@evansbrothers.co.uk) provides sound effects from each environment, as well as popular songs and rhymes that relate to outdoor exploration.

Areas of learning

Each **Out and About** title helps to support the following Foundation Stage areas of learning:
Personal, Social and Emotional Development
Communication, Language and Literacy
Mathematical Development
Knowledge and Understanding of the World
Physical Development
Creative Development

Making the most of reading time

When reading with younger children, take time to explore the pictures together. Ask children to find, identify, count or describe different objects. Point out colours and textures. Allow quiet spaces in your reading so that children can ask questions or repeat your words. Try pausing mid-sentence so that children can predict the next word. This sort of participation develops early reading skills.

Follow the words with your finger as you read. The main text is in Infant Sassoon, a clear, friendly font designed for children learning to read and write. The labels and sound effects add fun and give the opportunity to distinguish between levels of communication. Where appropriate, labels, sound effects or main text may be presented phonically. Encourage children to imitate the sounds.

As you read the book, you can also take the opportunity to talk about the book itself with appropriate vocabulary such as "page", "cover", "back", "front", "photograph", "label" and "page number".

You can also extend children's learning by using the books as a springboard for discussion and further activities. There are a few suggestions on the facing page.

Pages 4–5: Woodland visit

Take children on a woodland walk. Encourage them to draw (or photograph) all the things they can see and to describe the sounds and scents around them. You could also supervise children, one at a time, climbing over a sturdy tree trunk.

Pages 6–7: Changing seasons

Take children to a wood at different times of the year and help them to take photographs of a particular area. What do they notice has changed over time? Why do they think this is? You could also use photographs of your own, or from books or magazines, for an instant activity.

Pages 8–9: Look up!

Talk to children about the difference between deciduous and coniferous trees and why some leaves change colour and fall in the autumn. Encourage children to collect a selection of leaves. How many different colours and textures can the children describe? Use books or the Internet to help the children identify which trees the leaves come from.

Pages 10–11: On the ground

Draw pictures (or cut photographs from magazines) of woodland creatures and make a collage on the wall. Use a background of woodland colours and leaf patterns so that some of the creatures are camouflaged. How many creatures can the children find and identify? Talk to children about the way that camouflage is used for survival.

Pages 12–13: Tree textures

Encourage children to examine the bark of different types of trees (looking at sticks, branches and tree trunks). Show children how to count the rings on a fallen log to work out the age of the tree. Children may also enjoy doing some bark rubbings to compare tree textures.

Pages 14–15: Look inside!

Children may enjoy creating the sounds of woodland creatures using everyday materials, such as rustling (shaking a box of paper), hooting (using a comb and paper) or tapping (knocking a wood block). Encourage children to think about why a wood provides a good home for some animals.

Pages 16–17: Woodland home

Help children to make a small den or burrow of their own using old paper, sticks or leaves. Children may also enjoy playing a game about animals that use their ears to hunt at night. One child (the predator) is blindfolded and surrounded by a tight circle of children. Another child (the prey) answers the predator's call. The predator has to locate the child using sound alone.

Pages 18–19: Nuts and seeds

Take an old plastic box and, while wearing gloves, encourage children to collect items from the woodland floor (such as sticks, stones, moss, nuts and seeds). Warn children first about the dangers of fungi and poisonous berries. Encourage the children to create a miniature world – such as fairy or elf houses – from the materials they have found.

Pages 20–21: Using wood

Get involved with a tree planting campaign by planting seeds or trees in a wood in your area (see www.treeforall.org.uk for example). Encourage children to identify everyday items that are made from wood, such as pencils, paper, furniture and buildings. Children may also enjoy making some simple paper origami structures.

Index

Picture acknowledgements:
Alamy: 7 (Robert Stainforth); **Corbis:** 5 (Peter Carlsson/Etsa), 9 (Rick Gomez), 19 (Fancy/Veer), 21 (Jose Luis Pelaez, Inc); **Getty Images:** 8 (Anders Blomqvist), 10 (DKP), 12 (Sabine Fritsch/STOCK4B), 13 (Image Source), 20 (Tim Hall); **IStockphoto:** cover sky (JLFCapture); **Photolibrary:** 6 (James Frank), 15 (Robert Decells), 16 (Frank Lukasseck); **Shutterstock:** cover boy (Losevsky Pavel), cover leaves (Roman Sigaev), cover wood (Margaret Brudnicka), 2–3 leaves (Maksim Shmeljov), 4 (Monkey Business Images), 11 caterpillar (Joanna Zopoth-Lipiejko), 11 beetle (Galyna Andrushko), 11 snail (photoaloja), 11 ant (Kurt_G), 14 (Gertjan Hooijer), 17 owl (Alan Gleichman), 17 deer (Wayne James), 17 toad (Cheryl Casey), 17 snake (Lyle E. Doberstein), 18 (Daniel Hebert), 22–23 leaves (Maksim Shmeljov), 24 leaves (Maksim Shmeljov).